Cambridge **Discovery Education**™

▶ **INTERACTIVE READERS**

Series editor: Bob Hastings

LOSING IT
THE MEANING OF LOSS

B1

Brian Sargent

CAMBRIDGE UNIVERSITY PRESS
Cambridge, New York, Melbourne, Madrid, Cape Town,
Singapore, São Paulo, Delhi, Mexico City

Cambridge University Press
32 Avenue of the Americas, New York, NY 10013-2473, USA

www.cambridge.org
Information on this title: www.cambridge.org/9781107681910

First published 2014

Printed in Hong Kong, China, by Golden Cup Printing Company Limited

A catalog record for this publication is available from the British Library.

Library of Congress Cataloging-in-Publication Data

Sargent, Brian, 1969-
  Losing it : the meaning of loss / Brian Sargent.
      pages cm. -- (Cambridge discovery interactive readers)
  ISBN 978-1-107-68191-0 (pbk. : alk. paper)
  1. Loss (Psychology)--Juvenile literature. 2. English language--Textbooks for foreign speakers.
  3. Readers (Elementary) I. Title.

BF575.D35S28 2013
155.9'3--dc23

                            2013018631

ISBN 978-1-107-68191-0

Additional resources for this publication at www.cambridge.org

Layout services, art direction, book design, and photo research: Q2ABillSMITH GROUP
Editorial services: Hyphen S.A.
Audio production: CityVox, New York
Video production: Q2ABillSMITH GROUP

Contents

Before You Read:
Get Ready!

Imagine you are lost at sea with no food and no water. What can you do to survive? How long do you think you can live? Three boys face this problem in this book. Read on to find out more!

Words to Know

Match the definition to the highlighted word in each sentence.

1 You may find many animal species on a farm, including cows and chickens. ___

2 Most plants cannot survive without water. ___

3 The car stopped when it had no more fuel. ___

4 Nobody knows the location of the lost children. ___

a something burned to make heat or power

b a group of similar animals or plants

c continue to live

d the place something can be found

Words to Know

Read the paragraph, then check (✓) the true sentence.

In the 1800s, there were millions of passenger pigeons living all over North America. By 1914, there was only one: a passenger pigeon named Martha. Martha lived at a zoo in Cincinnati, Ohio, and was the last living passenger pigeon in the world. On September 1, 1914, Martha died. Passenger pigeons had become extinct.

a ___ When an animal dies in a zoo, the species is extinct.

b ___ When a species is extinct, that means it no longer exists.

c ___ A species is extinct when they are very difficult to find.

Science Words to Know

Read the definitions and then complete the sentences.

Science words!

Everything in the world is made up of very small things called *atoms*.

Gravity is the natural force that makes things fall down.

A *black hole* is an area in space where gravity is so strong that nothing, not even light, can get away from it.

A *satellite* is a special machine that travels around Earth.

A *fossil* is a part of a plant or animal, or its shape that has been saved in rock or in the ground for a very long time.

1 The star was pulled in by the _____.

2 A bone of dead dinosaurs is a _____.

3 The story says that Newton discovered _____ when an apple fell on his head.

4 There are millions of _____ in a human body.

5 Sputnik was the first _____ ever sent into space.

CHAPTER 1

Lost (and Found)

WHAT DOES IT MEAN "TO BE LOST"?

Every year people lose things on public transportation in London—the city's buses, taxis, and subways. But 2011 was especially bad. Transport for London, which runs London's public transportation system, collected over 207,000 lost things that year. It was a new record.

Most of the lost things Transport for London collects are never claimed[1] by their owners. Only about one third of the things find their owners again. The rest are given away, sold, or recycled.[2] And some of them go to an art gallery.

[1] **claim:** ask for something because it belongs to you
[2] **recycle:** use something again

In 2011, Transport for London **searched** through their collection of lost things. They were looking for art. They found paintings, drawings, photos, and other pieces. They took about 60 interesting pieces of art and put on an art show. The show was called "The Lost Collection." None of the pieces had a signature.

Think about an art show of lost art. What is each piece about? Who were the artists? How did they feel about the work? How did they feel about losing their art? Is the work even finished? The Lost Collection invited people to think about these questions.

The word "lost" has many meanings. You can lose a piece of art, but you can also lose your mind. To lose your mind means "to go crazy." Both art and minds can be lost on a subway, but only one can be collected and taken to a "lost and found" office!

Is losing always a bad thing? People are usually happy when they lose weight. You can even lose yourself in a book, meaning you enjoy it very much. Of course, you can also get lost in real life. That means you no longer know where you are or which way to go, which may not be so pleasant.

? EVALUATE

What do you think about Transport for London's art show? How would you feel if you found your art in the show?

CHAPTER 2

The Biggest Loser

SOMETIMES IT'S THE LOSERS WHO END UP WINNING.

On April 11, 2001, the small Pacific island nation of American Samoa met Australia in a FIFA soccer match. FIFA is the organization that runs soccer's World Cup. Nobody expected the game would be close. Because of passport problems, most of American Samoa's team was not there. From the original 20-player group, only the goalkeeper had made it. The rest of the team was filled with new players. Some were only 15 years old, and most had never played a full 90-minute competitive game before.

American Samoa lost 31 to 0. It was the biggest loss[3] in FIFA history.

What did the American Samoa team do after losing so badly? They sang. They put their arms around each other and sang to the crowd.

[3] **loss:** the action of losing

David Smith, the Samoan's Australian representative,[4] said later, "They are fantastic singers. If it was a singing competition, everyone else would have given up by now. Great people, great voices, but they just can't play."

Losing is a part of sports. In almost all competitions, there must be a loser. Most of the time, the loser leaves the field quickly while the winner stays and celebrates. But sometimes, as with American Samoa's wonderful singers, the loser is the important story.

One of the most famous losses of all time didn't take place in the world of sports but in the world of **war**. In 480 BCE, Greece was at war with Persia. King Xerxes I of Persia set out with a very large army to control all of Greece. Historians from the time said the Persian army had over one million **soldiers**, but modern writers say the number was probably lower – between 100,000 and 360,000.

[4]**representative:** someone who speaks for another person or group

Xerxes led the Persian army to Thermopylae. Thermopylae was a narrow path in central Greece. Only a few people could travel on the path at one time. On one side of the path was the sea and on the other side were tall mountains. To meet them at Thermopylae, King Leonidas of Sparta took an army of only about seven thousand soldiers.

The Persian army had far more soldiers than the Spartan army. The Persian army was like a large, traveling city! When Xerxes sent someone to speak with King Leonidas, he offered them friendship and better lands if they allowed the Persian army to pass. If not, however, he promised his army would shoot so many arrows, the Spartans would not be able to see the sun. Leonidas did not agree to let the Persians through, and the fighting began.

The Spartans stopped the Persian army for seven days. On the seventh day, the Persian army found a secret way over the mountains and around the Spartans. When Leonidas learned the Persians had gone around them, he sent most of his small army away. He stayed, along with just a few hundred soldiers. They fought while the rest of his army traveled back to Greece to fight another day.

Even though the Greeks lost the battle of Thermopylae, they later won the war. Though the Persian army did control much of Greece, Xerxes had to return home to stop problems in his own lands. The small army he left in Greece lost, and the war for control of the land ended.

?

ANALYZE

Why do you think King Leonidas did not accept Xerxes' offer of friendship and land?

Spartans and Persians used arrows when they fought one another at the battle of Thermopylae.

Land of the Lost

MILLIONS OF YEARS AGO, THE WORLD WAS A VERY DIFFERENT PLACE. WHAT WILL CHANGE IN THE NEXT MILLION YEARS?

In Arkansas in 2004, Gene Sparling was kayaking through a swamp when he saw a bird. This is not unusual. However, when Sparling told people about it, they became very excited. The bird may have been an Ivory-billed Woodpecker. Most people believed that Ivory-billed Woodpeckers were **extinct**.

In the late 1800s and early 1900s, people cut down the forests in the Southeastern United States where the Ivory-billed Woodpecker lived. Over time, people saw fewer and fewer of the birds. Then, when all the forests were gone, the bird was gone, too. After 1944, no one saw any more Ivory-billed Woodpeckers.

Sixty years later, no one is certain. After 2004, people hurried to the **location** where Sparling had seen the woodpecker. Some of them said they also saw it. Others searched for years and did not. So is the Ivory-billed Woodpecker extinct? The answer depends on whom you ask.

Animals are becoming extinct all around the world. As the human population grows, many animal populations are getting smaller. Scientists believe thousands of animal **species** become extinct every year. There are now hundreds of thousands of animal species in danger of extinction. Some of the most famous animals in danger are tigers, rhinoceroses, and gorillas.

Certainly, the most famous extinct animals ever are the dinosaurs. They are so famous, we see them everywhere. They are in movies and on television. Children play with dinosaur toys and carry their lunch in dinosaur lunch boxes. But how is it that everyone knows what dinosaurs look like? No one has ever seen one alive.

Video Quest

Orangutans

Why are orangutans a common target for illegal wildlife trade?

The word dinosaur means "terrible lizard." Although dinosaurs were not lizards, some were truly terrible. The Spinosaurus was usually 15 meters long, but sometimes as long as 18 meters and had a mouth full of razor-sharp teeth. The Argentinosaurus weighed as much as 100 cars and had a neck so long, it could look into a fourth-floor window.

But you won't find an Argentinosaurus looking in your window today. About 65 million years ago, all the dinosaurs became extinct. Everything we know about dinosaurs is from their **fossils**. There are many different kinds of fossils. Dinosaur fossils are often stone copies of their bones. These fossils are made when the bones of dead dinosaurs under the ground slowly become stone. It can take hundreds of years for a fossil to form.

Paleontologists are scientists who study fossils. Using fossils, paleontologists imagine the lost world of the dinosaurs. They form ideas about the dinosaur's appearance, where it lived, and even what food it ate. However, it is not an easy job.

Imagine you are a paleontologist. You find some dinosaur fossils. Could you make a dinosaur from them? First, you must answer many difficult questions:

- Do you have all the fossils you need?
  Sometimes paleontologists must imagine a dinosaur from only a few parts. The giant Argentinosaurus was formed and named after only a few bones were found. One was a shoulder bone bigger than a car!

- Do you have fossils from different dinosaurs mixed together?
  One of the biggest dinosaur mistakes was made putting the Brontosaurus together. One paleontologist put the head of one dinosaur on the body of another.

- How do the fossils fit together?
  In 1868, a paleontologist famously put the head of the Elasmosaurus at the end of its tail.

CHAPTER 4

Lost at Sea

TWO-THIRDS OF THE EARTH IS OCEAN. COULD YOU SURVIVE BEING LOST AT SEA?

In October 2010, three boys climbed into a small boat and traveled out to sea. One boy was 14 years old. The other two were 15. The boat they took was not theirs, and they didn't tell anyone where they were going.

The boys lived on a small island in the Pacific Ocean between New Zealand and Hawaii. They were planning on visiting another island about 70 kilometers away. For their trip, they packed 20 coconuts to eat. Halfway to their destination, the boat ran out of gas.

The boys floated out to sea. They ate all the coconuts in the first two days. So the boys caught fish to eat and carefully collected rain water to drink. Every drop was important. When bad weather came, the boys lay flat on the bottom of the little boat so it didn't turn over.

The boys were lost at sea for over seven weeks. Two weeks before they were found, their family and friends had a memorial service[5] for them. Over one third of the people of the nearby islands came to the service. At about the same time, the three boys in the boat caught and ate a sea bird.

On the 50th day, the boys were 1,400 kilometers from their home island when a man on a fishing boat saw them. "The boys looked very bad," fisherman Tai Fredricsen said. At first, the boys could not drink. They put water in their mouths and held it there for 30 minutes. Finally, they were able to swallow.[6] Four hours later, they were eating slices of fruit and resting in Fredricsen's bed. The three boys were so thin, they all fit into the bed easily. When Fredricsen spoke with newspapers afterwards, he said the boys smiled the whole time. They had **survived**.

[5]**memorial service:** an event in the name of someone who has died
[6]**swallow:** move food or liquid from your mouth into your stomach

Many stories like this do not have happy endings. The Earth's oceans are very large. Things lost in the ocean often never get found. There is one area of the Atlantic Ocean that is famous for this. It's called the Bermuda Triangle.[7]

The Bermuda Triangle is over a million square kilometers of ocean to the east of the United States of America. It is famous because some people believe that an unusual number of things have been lost inside the triangle. Some say over 50 ships and 20 planes have been lost there.

In 1918, the ship USS *Cyclops* sank in the Bermuda Triangle and 309 people were lost.

....

[7]**triangle:** a shape with three sides

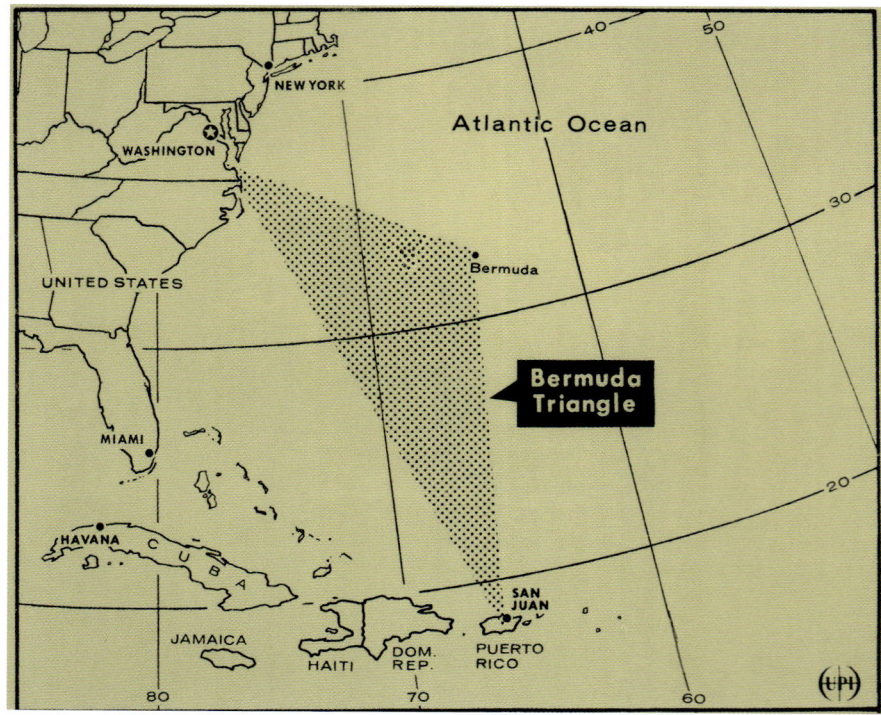

In 1945, five military planes flying together disappeared over the triangle. The planes were never found and no one knows why they disappeared. These and many other ships and planes have been lost inside the triangle.

Five military planes flying together

People have written books and made movies about the Bermuda Triangle. They call the area "mysterious" because no one can explain why so many things disappear there. Some say magic is the reason. Others think aliens[8] are responsible. However, scientists believe there is nothing special at all about the site. They say that the number of ships and planes lost in the triangle is not unusual. The mystery, they say, is all in people's imagination.

....

[8]**alien:** a living thing from another planet

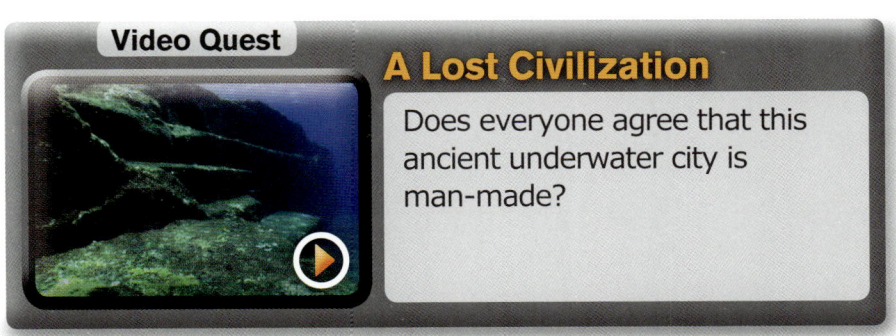

Video Quest

A Lost Civilization

Does everyone agree that this ancient underwater city is man-made?

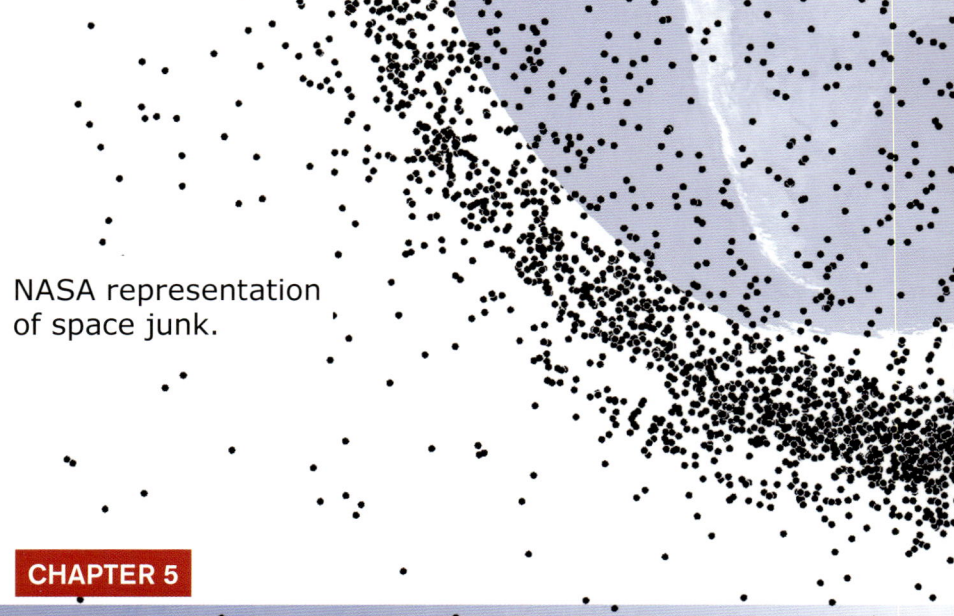

NASA representation of space junk.

CHAPTER 5

Lost in Space

LOOK UP! SPACE IS FILLED WITH LOST THINGS.

Can you lose a satellite the size of a bus? The answer is "yes and no." In 2005, NASA, the organization that runs the United States' space program, lost their UARS satellite. However, they knew exactly where it was.

To lose a satellite usually means that they no longer have control of it. In this case, the UARS satellite ran out of fuel. The satellite was in orbit around Earth, which means it was traveling at a very high speed around the planet. When it ran out of fuel, it still continued to orbit the Earth. So the satellite was lost, even though NASA knew where it was.

UARS was not alone. There are many lost satellites orbiting Earth and we know the location of every one. A US organization called the Space Surveillance Network watches every lost satellite in orbit. Sometimes these lost satellites crash into each other and break into pieces. The Space Surveillance Network watches those pieces, too. All together, there are about 18,000 man-made things in orbit. We know exactly where they all are and where they are going, but we can't control them.

Of the 18,000 things in orbit, only about 900 are working satellites. The rest is just space junk.[9] Over time, most space junk will fall out of orbit and come down to Earth. In 2011, that's what the UARS satellite did. Most of the satellite burned up as it fell. The rest almost certainly crashed into the ocean.

[9]**junk:** trash or something with little value

Satellites are not the only things to get lost in space. In 2005, there were nine planets in our solar system. By 2006, there were only eight. The planet we lost was Pluto. Of course, we didn't exactly lose it. Pluto is still there, but it is no longer a planet. Astronomers, the scientists who study space and planets, decided that Pluto was too small and too far away from our sun to be called a planet. Instead, it is now called a dwarf planet, which means a small planet.

So what does it take to become truly lost in space? It may take something called a **black hole**. Black holes are difficult to explain. They exist in space, but no one has ever seen them. We can, however, see what black holes do to the things around them.

A black hole is a place in space where **gravity** is very strong. Black holes have a lot of mass,[10] but they can be very small. Scientists believe the smallest black hole may be the size of an atom but have the mass of a small mountain. The largest black holes, called supermassive black holes, are the size of over a million Earths and have a mass greater than many million Suns.

Because a black hole's gravity is so strong, something pulled into it is lost forever. Even light is pulled in. Black holes can also pull in larger things, such as planets or stars. Recently, astronomers watched a star falling into a black hole. It took 15 months for the star to fall in completely. This black hole is about three billion light-years[11] away from the Earth, so the astronomers were watching something which happened a long time ago.

[10] **mass:** the amount of matter in an object
[11] **light-year:** the distance light travels in one year (about 9,460,000,000,000 kilometers)

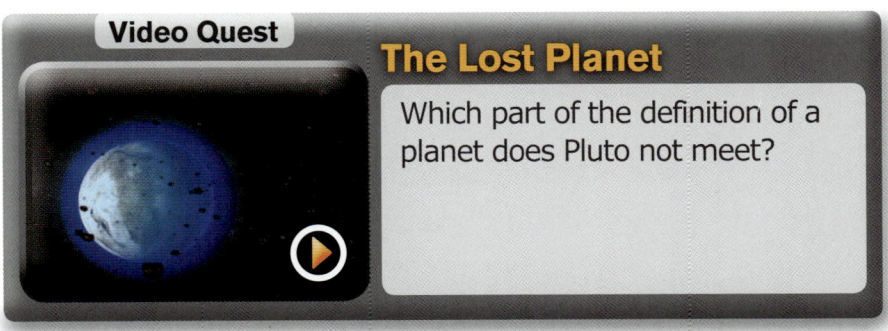

Video Quest

The Lost Planet

Which part of the definition of a planet does Pluto not meet?

CHAPTER 6

What Do You Think?

WHAT IS THE DIFFERENCE BETWEEN WINNING AND LOSING? ONE AMERICAN WRITER BELIEVES LOSING TEACHES YOU MORE.

American writer Pat Conroy once wrote a book called *My Losing Season*. It tells the story of Conroy's love for basketball. Interestingly, he didn't write about winning, he wrote about losing.

People learn more from losing than they can from winning, Conroy says in his book. Winning feels great, but you do not learn anything from it. When you lose, you often take time to understand why. Losing invites you to think and explore the reasons for the loss. You think about what you did wrong. You think about what you can do differently in the future.

Do you agree? Think about your wins and losses. Which one taught you more? Think about this quote from Conroy's book: "Loss follows you home and taunts[12] you at the breakfast table, follows you to work in the morning." Have you ever experienced this feeling? If so, what happened? What did you do?

If losing is important, then knowing how to lose must also be important. Have you ever heard someone called a sore loser? That is a person who loses and acts very badly because of it. But a good loser is a person who loses but does not act badly. In Chapter 2 of this book, the American Samoan soccer players were good losers. They lost very badly, yet they sang to the crowd afterwards. Why do you think they did that?

How do you act when you lose? Are you a sore loser? Do you become angry? Or are you a good loser, and congratulate[13] the other team? What do you think it means to be a good loser?

....

[12]**taunt:** say unkind things about someone to make them angry
[13]**congratulate:** tell someone you are happy because they did something good

After You Read

Read the sentences and choose Ⓐ (True) or Ⓑ (False).

1 Most of the things lost on London's subways, taxis, and buses are claimed by their owners.

Ⓐ True
Ⓑ False

2 After the Greeks lost the battle of Thermopylae, they lost the war against Persia.

Ⓐ True
Ⓑ False

3 Paleontologists study fossils to form ideas about how dinosaurs looked.

Ⓐ True
Ⓑ False

4 No one can survive being lost at sea for 50 days.

Ⓐ True
Ⓑ False

5 Scientists believe that the Bermuda Triangle is not a mysterious area at all.

Ⓐ True
Ⓑ False

6 It is impossible to know the location of a lost satellite.

Ⓐ True
Ⓑ False

7 Black holes can pull in planets and stars.

Ⓐ True
Ⓑ False

Match

Choose the best match for each sentence.

1 lose your mind _____

2 lose your way _____

3 lose weight _____

4 lose yourself in a book _____

a become thinner
b not know what direction to go
c enjoy reading it very much
d go crazy

Choose the Correct Answers

Read the following sentences and choose Ⓐ , Ⓑ , or Ⓒ.

1 To survive on the sea, the three lost boys _____.

   Ⓐ swam to the nearest island

   Ⓑ drank rain water and caught fish

   Ⓒ called for help on their radio

2 Scientists believe _____ species become extinct every year.

   Ⓐ a few

   Ⓑ hundreds of

   Ⓒ thousands of

?

EVALUATE

Many of the man-made things orbiting Earth are space junk. What is the problem with so much space junk?

Answer Key

Words to Know, page 4
1 b **2** c **3** a **4** d

Words to Know, page 4
b

Words to Know, page 5
1 black hole **2** fossil **3** gravity **4** atoms **5** satellite

Evaluate, page 7   *Answers will vary.*

Analyze, page 11   *Answers will vary.*

Video Quest, page 13
Orangutans are large and slow, so they are easy to catch. Females are the most popular for hunters who hope to catch them with their young. Orangutans are often sold as pets.

Video Quest, page 19
No. Some people think the city was formed naturally.

Video Quest, page 23
Pluto does not fit the definition of a planet because it is not big enough to push other objects in its orbit out of its way.

True or False, page 26
1 B **2** B **3** A **4** B **5** A **6** B **7** A

Match, page 26
1 d **2** b **3** a **4** c

Choose the Correct Answers, page 27
1 B **2** C

Evaluate, page 27   *Answers will vary.*